MW01063261

101 USES FOR A CHIHUAHUA

Published by Willow Creek Press, Inc.
P.O. Box 147, Minocqua, Wisconsin 54548

All Photos © agefotostock

Design: Donnie Rubo
Printed in China

101 USES FOR A CHIHUAHUA

WILLOW CREEK PRESS®

Spy

Snuggle Buddy

Lunch Date

Laundry Helper

Bookworm

Tutor

Scholar

Fabric Softener

Skateboarder

Dietitian

Deodorizer

Escort

Superhero Sidekick

Groundskeeper

First Mate

Personal Shopper

Confidant

Garden Gnome

Security Alarm

Bed Warmer

Q-tip

Moist Towelette

Seat Warmer

Measuring Stick

Kitchen Helper

Playmate

Farmhand

Cowboy

Herder

Neighborhood Watch

Bookends

Babysitter

Sous Chef

Nanny

Washcloth

Supermodel

Centerfold

Diva

Fashion Accessory

Food Critic

Dishwasher

Santa's Elf

Present   # Stocking-stuffer

Hide & Seek Partner

Trendsetter

Wilderness Guide

Clown

Bucket of Laughs

Welcoming Committee

Florist

GPS

Blogger   **Dance Partner**

Lookout

Trainee　　　　　**Bodyguard**

Band Member

Executive Assistant

Cheerleader

Sun Dial

Comedian

Alarm Clock

Agility Trainer

Pilot

Garbage Disposal

Botanist

Harvester

Facebook Friend

Cobbler

Fashionista

Roommate

Personal Trainer

Best Friends

Chauffeur

High Jumper

Pedometer

Chick Magnet

Stuffed Animal

Teammates

Long-Distance Runner

Sprinter

Hurdler

Party Planner

Beach Bum

Lifeguard

Ballplayer

Stowaway

Daredevil

Gardener

Landscaper

Romantic

Flirt

Editor

I.T. Support

Contractor

Accountant

Snowplow

Chest Protector

Trailblazer

Scarf